For a Tax-Free Green Transition

A parallel economy revolving around its own currency!

References for the data:

References for the data can be verified by conducting an online search using the keywords mentioned in the text, enabling easy fact-checking. For further inquiries, the author can be contacted through the website findtheflaw.com.

Acknowledgments:

This English translation was made possible thanks to the thoughtful editing of Margaret Strubel.

For a Tax-Free Green Transition

Essay

Vincent Lannoye

For a Tax-Free Green Transition
Copyright © Vincent Lannoye 2022 (with December 2025 edits)
All rights reserved. No part of this publication may be reproduced, stored in a retrieval system, or transmitted in any form or by any means, electronic, mechanical, photocopying, recording, or otherwise, without written permission of the copyright holder.
ISBN-13: 9798841632566

This present book is based on:
The History of Money for Understanding Economics
Copyright © 2015 Vincent Lannoye

In memory of my mother.

Table of Contents

Introduction
Prerequisite: No Easy Solution in Sight

1. A Tax-Free Parallel Market for Higher Wages................13
A new tax-free market outside of the regular and black markets
A green-currency exclusively in green-accounts
Creation of green-dollars by the banking system
Control of the green-accounts of voluntary green-corporations
No control for green-wage earners
The rest of the economy unaffected
Tax-free green-products
Tax-free green products: Prices possibly down 50%
Green-jobs and higher wages
No more complex than the regular economy
Tax-free: Minimal impact on the Treasury

2. A New Gray-Money to Supervise the Green-Market.............24
A new gray-money within green-accounts
Introduction of gray-cents
Tracking fossil fuel consumption with gray-cents for voluntary corporations
Easier control of green-corporations: Gray-cents fit perfectly with green-money
Gray-cents for individuals: Eye-opening
Ratcheting up the tax in gray-cents? Maybe never

3. Make the Rich Pay More................29
Quotas of gray-cents
Quotas on consumption items and long-term assets
Monitoring cash withdrawals from regular accounts
Corporations: Just passing it on to consumers
A market for unused quotas: make the rich pay
Incentivizing participation: A $1,000 monthly bonus

Conclusion: *A Monetary Solution to Reduce Inequalities and Contain Global Warming?*

Bibliography
Origin of illustrations:

Introduction

Parallel markets and alternative currencies have existed throughout history. In times of crisis, they've often provided vital support—especially when official systems failed or governments became oppressive, as seen with black markets.

Drawing on these historical examples, this book introduces a new idea: the *Green-Market System*. It proposes a parallel currency aimed at reducing inequality and helping to address climate change. Could this bold solution offer a way forward?

This book is the final chapter of "The History of Money for Understanding Economics," which covers key topics such as money, loans, banking, monetary creation, inflation, the Federal Reserve, black markets, and the many transformations of the monetary system. These concepts are not explained in detail here.

For readers seeking a deeper understanding of how monetary systems work, the full version of the original book is referenced in the accompanying image.

Prerequisite:
No Easy Solution in Sight

FIGHTING GLOBAL WARMING

PROBLEMATIC ECONOMIC IMPLICATIONS

+ A parallel market to bypass political deadlock
Vincent Lannoye

Inequality and global warming are the two armies launching a pincer movement on a society polarized about the strategy.

In the context of persistent inequality, low-income workers are rejecting the establishment and its green agenda, demanding a focus on domestic job creation and wage increases.

Concerning global warming, the younger generation is challenging free-market capitalism that relies on cheap energy, leaning towards progressive and even socialist ideologies.

As a prerequisite for this chapter, the book "Fighting Global Warming: Problematic economic implications" cautions against demagogic solutions. It argues that government intervention has limited impact; real progress depends on new technologies and the private sector to create jobs, including green jobs. To date, the government has not found a way to accelerate this growth effectively. There is no "magic mix" of regulations and taxation that can resolve these issues of low wages and global warming, leaving the government unable to take decisive action beyond implementing symbolic minimum wages and engaging in superficial greenwashing.

1. A Tax-Free Parallel Market for Higher Wages

A new tax-free market outside of the regular and black markets

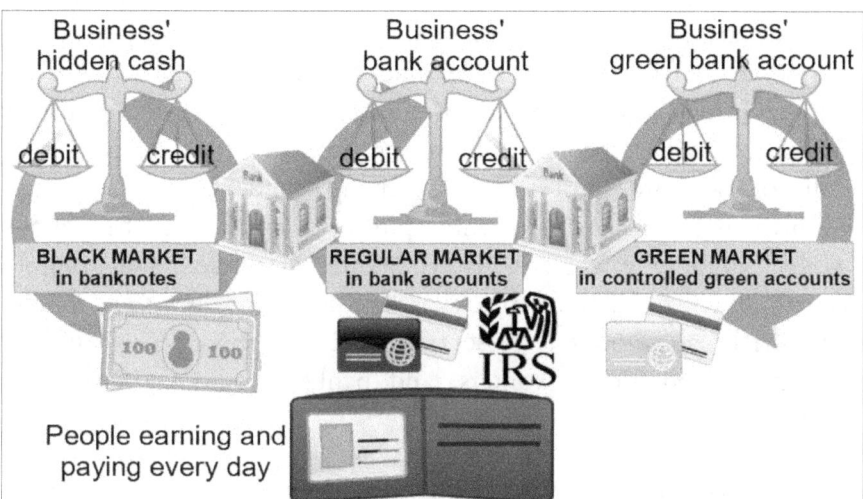

The next pages, based on the drawing above, will examine the feasibility of establishing a new market outside the regular economy and away from the black market.

The preliminary condition is to isolate this new market from the existing markets. It hinges on confining the new market within its own accounting framework.

The final steps will aim to attract individuals, investors, businesses, and perhaps workers displaced by AI to this new market, and to encourage Congress to adopt it.

Economists often overlook the existence of a parallel black market, which is estimated to generate $2 trillion annually in the US and an even larger share of GDP in some other countries. While addressing international crime and illicit financial flows is important, the black market also serves as a source of employment, often offering competitive wages, particularly to low-income workers. In some cases, it provides a crucial economic lifeline for marginalized individuals in authoritarian or corrupt nations. This underground economy primarily operates in cash to evade detection and relies on hidden accounting systems. For a more detailed analysis, see *The History of Money for Understanding Economics*, from which this chapter was extracted.

Similar to the black market but operating legally, could a new tax-exempt market be established? This market would operate independently from the conventional taxed economy while remaining distinct from the illicit black market. In other words, it would require separate accounting systems, distinct from both the regular economy and the black market.

To encourage participation, this framework would eliminate all forms of taxation—including income, corporate, sales, and potentially payroll taxes. At the same time, like the black market, it should generate investment returns and well-paying jobs. Motivation among participants is key: people need strong incentives to take part, and profits or wages are essential for any thriving economy.

This new parallel market could aptly be referred to as the "*green-market*," alluding to its black-market counterpart while highlighting its "green" content. Unlike the black market, however, this system should serve the broader interests of society. All its components—including products, corporations, workers, and banks—would be labeled as "*green.*"

A green-currency exclusively in green-accounts

To isolate the green-market, a distinct digital currency, supported by banking controls, could ensure the market's full segregation from the regular dollars. This currency would exist exclusively in electronic form within bank accounts, with no option for withdrawal in physical banknotes. Such a specialized currency could be termed "green-currency," "green-money," or "green-dollar."

Implementing such a digital-only currency would enable the precise supervision of banking transactions in green-accounts, similar to how banks currently filter out terrorism-related and illicit activities. This digital control would protect the tax-exempt green economy, which is dedicated exclusively to the production and trade of green-products and green-services, avoiding polluting regular products and prohibited drugs. The tax-exempt status is granted in exchange for stringent controls.

The green-money accounts should not overwhelm banks and payment processing companies, as they already manage foreign currencies. Many banks are experienced in handling deposits and loans in both dollars and euros for their corporate clients. Their existing banking software would only require minor adjustments, such as adding a new green-dollar sign alongside the traditional dollar sign ($) and the euro sign (€).

This form of tax shielding through currency would be simpler than bureaucratic controls involving subsidies or tax breaks. A tax-free parallel market with its own currency could easily accommodate existing companies that cannot always operate under complex tax rules or within the confines of a tax-free restricted zone near a remote coastal harbor.

Criminal activities are likely to continue using gold coins or physical banknotes, as illustrated in the image, to evade the banking oversight imposed by authorities on dollar transactions.

Remarkably, such illicit cash flows CANNOT mingle with a secondary, voluntary, tax-free green-currency that is fully recorded in bank accounts. Criminals will avoid the green-market and its banking controls. Instead, they will remain in their black market, using exclusively gold coins or paper banknotes of the regular currency. This avoidance principle serves as the cornerstone of the green-market: establishing a parallel digital-only currency COULD separate the accounting of the new green economy from both the regular and black markets.

Creation of green-dollars by the banking system

To initiate the creation of green-dollars, Congress would authorize a conversion mechanism between regular dollars and green-dollars at the Federal Reserve, with both currencies pegged at par for exchange purposes. This exchange would be akin to the historical conversion of dollar bills into gold coins. In this way, the total money supply—the sum of ordinary dollars and green-dollars—would not initially change.

Banking institutions would then be able to convert regular dollars into green-dollars at the Fed. Under supervision, they could also exchange ordinary dollars for green-dollars among themselves on the foreign exchange market, notifying the Fed but without going directly through its facilities.

Banks would then offer deposit and credit accounts denominated in green-dollars. Companies engaged in green activities, as well as individuals, could receive loans denominated in this currency.

Control of the green-accounts of voluntary green-corporations

Authorized green-corporations would open green deposit and credit accounts. They would conduct all transactions exclusively through these green-accounts using the green-currency, ensuring a self-contained system. Green-corporations would pay green-dollars to a provider's regular dollar account to purchase from the regular economy; the payment system would automatically convert these funds into the currency of the receiving accounts. In the opposite direction, green-corporations could receive regular dollars immediately converted into green-dollars as payment for the sale of green-products. In this manner, the two markets could interact and trade much like neighboring countries, with currency exchanges at the border.

These green-accounts would always be subject to rigorous audits to verify that tax-exempt payments and income are directly tied to the production of approved green-products. Green-banks would scrutinize these transactions before authorizing the conversion and transfer of green-dollars into regular dollar accounts. Oversight of green-accounts would detect irregularities such as unusual gas consumption or unjustified tax-exempt labor. Regulatory auditors could compare corporate metrics related to raw materials, supplier inputs, and workforce levels against average ratios observed in the green-accounts of industry peers.

Green-corporations can benefit from tax-exempt status, but this privilege must be subject to strict oversight to ensure transparency and adherence to the system's guidelines. Only voluntary green-corporations would have their green-accounts subject to supplementary audits, ensuring transparency and compliance within the green-market. Such robust regulatory systems already exist for other corporations going public in the stock market, requiring frequent auditing by firms such as Deloitte or KPMG.

No control for green-wage earners

Green-wages would be exempt from direct controls, as the green-money paid by employers would already have undergone clearance procedures at the corporate level. Green-workers would accept green-wages if the compensation is favorable compared with net wages in the regular economy. Their earnings would be credited to their green-accounts.

Green-workers could spend their wages on green-products or exchange their green-dollars for regular dollars at their bank whenever they wish. For holders of green-accounts, transactions involving the exchange of green-dollars and regular dollars would resemble credit-card payments in foreign currencies, with only a single transaction line appearing in their respective bank statements.

Alternatively, green-workers could choose to save their earnings in green-accounts, allowing banks to invest these funds within the green market. They could also invest their green-dollars in green-corporations, keeping capital circulating within the system. The same approach would apply to shareholders of green-corporations, who could reinvest their tax-free dividends, further supporting growth and sustainability within the green-economy.

Regular households could as well legally earn tax-free green-dollars through side jobs within the green-market. For instance, they could install solar panels on their residential roofs and sell the electricity to a green-electricity distributor, with controls applied seamlessly through the green-corporation's green-account. Their extra tax-free income in green-currency could be spent on other green-products, invested in green-corporations, or simply exchanged for regular dollars. This concept is similar in structure to the black market, where individuals participate informally for a few hours a week outside their primary employment—though here it would occur within a fully legal framework.

The rest of the economy unaffected

The stringent oversight within the green-market would not affect the regular producers and consumers of conventional taxable goods paid in regular currency, as only the voluntary green-corporations within the green-market would be subject to close regulatory scrutiny.

Any criminal or underground transactions will continue to use regular dollar banknotes. Such activities must avoid the voluntary green-currency, which is fully traceable by auditors due to its digital nature and mandatory recording in bank accounts.

Meanwhile, the IRS would continue to tax traditional incomes in regular currency, while maintaining its vigilance in identifying illicit transactions within conventional bank accounts.

Tax-free green-products

The affordability of green products should increase due to their lower tax-free prices, which would expand the range of buyers. Economies of scale should then drive prices down even further, enabling more consumers to purchase an increasing number of green products.

Potential green-products and green-services could include:
- power plants with solar panels or wind turbines;
- solar panels installation on residential rooftops;
- timber for housing, aimed at CO_2 sequestration;
- battery packs;
- heat pump manufacturing and installation;
- carbon removal products;
- nuclear power plants for electricity providers;
- components for all green-products listed above, potentially supplied by new green subsidiaries of existing corporations.

Will prices of green products decrease if taxes are eliminated? Yes, they should, driven by competitive dynamics among providers striving to increase their market share by offering lower prices.

This economic competition will, of course, require a vigilant consumer base ready to take legal action against corporations engaging in price fixing or violating antitrust laws, reminiscent of the 1907 Roosevelt vs. Paper Trust case. Equally crucial is the role of a free and investigative press capable of exposing unethical activities, whether perpetrated by greedy CEOs or corrupt politicians. Most importantly, the best safeguard against inflated prices is a vibrant startup ecosystem ready to challenge larger corporations with competitive pricing. Individual responsibility remains an indispensable factor, as in any democratic society that champions free markets.

Tax-free green products: Prices possibly down 50%

A myriad of taxes end up in the final price of all product categories, including green products. This means that consumers of clean energy and green alternatives pay for the sales tax (direct taxation), but they also pay for prices that must incorporate custom tolls, income taxes on the workers building the wind turbines or solar panels, income taxes of part suppliers, permit fees for installation, and more (indirect taxation). All taxes and fees invariably contribute to the final prices paid by consumers. This overall taxation on all products is higher than generally perceived.

On average, taxes in the US account for approximately 28% of GDP, based on the tax-to-GDP ratio, which includes federal, state, county, and municipal taxes but excludes Social Security taxes, as they are not factored into GDP calculations. In some European countries, this tax burden can reach up to 45% of GDP, according to international tax-to-GDP measurements.

Since household consumption makes up about 70% of US GDP, the tax-to-GDP ratio provides insight into the portion of selling prices that reflects taxation. However, the actual tax component in selling prices varies. It can be close to zero for free public services like roads, relatively low for subsidized goods and services, or significantly higher for products and services with high labor costs. For instance, in the US, consumption products that rely heavily on highly paid engineers may have an effective tax burden of up to 50%, while in the EU, this could reach 60%. The taxes collected from these higher-cost goods ultimately help fund essential public services such as infrastructure and education.

Taxes are not always paid by the rich to benefit the poor; in many cases, the distribution of tax burdens and benefits is more intricate. Any form of taxation can potentially affect the poor more than the rich. For example, sales taxes disproportionately burden low-income individuals because they consume a higher share of their income, whereas higher-income individuals spend a smaller proportion. This regressive nature of sales taxes is widely acknowledged by economists, which is why most US states exempt groceries from them.

*Income tax presents a more complex scenario. Raising the tax rates of the highest tax brackets may target high-wage earners and corporations, but the indirect tax burden (or "**tax incidence**") can shift to consumers. If individual or corporate suppliers pass on the cost of income taxes through higher prices, both low- and high-income individuals bear part of the burden.*

The black market reinforces the observation that the income tax burden falls on consumers as well as suppliers. Black-market consumers and providers typically negotiate to share the tax savings compared to the selling price in the formal economy, which includes all forms of taxation. These savings include any income or corporate taxes that are omitted from black-market invoices. As a result, black-market consumers benefit from lower costs due to the absence of income taxation, whereas in the formal economy the same purchase would place the full tax liability of the regular market price on the buyer. This illustrates that the incidence of income tax is shared between consumers and providers, rather than falling solely on corporate or individual providers.

Such a dynamic should encourage a thoughtful examination of how a tax-free parallel economy, akin to the black market, could help reduce costs for low-income consumers.

Green-jobs and higher wages

Lower prices would attract more buyers in the tax-free green-market. This growth would encourage greater corporate participation, creating more job opportunities for all workers, including those with lower incomes. Employers may need to offer competitive wages—either as net wages in the green-market or as gross wages in the regular economy that yield an equivalent take-home pay.

The increase in net wages would not come directly from tax savings on green wages, as only selling prices would reflect those savings. Instead, wage growth would be driven by overall market expansion, with employers competing for workers by offering higher net wages in the green market or higher gross wages in the traditional economy.

Other regulations and taxation policies should be implemented with caution. As discussed in "Inequality and Economic Policies: Just tax the rich?," governments have tried numerous subsidy programs over recent decades, but many have underperformed due to excessive complexity and poor follow-up after implementation.

Given this, the green-market presents a viable alternative with the potential to stimulate job growth and increase wages. Moreover, further benefits could help reduce inequality and address global warming, as explored in the following pages.

No more complex than the regular economy

The green-market system would not be more complicated than today's economy. It would simply be another financial tool to manage, much like tracking work hours or managing standard accounting tasks. This system would be neither more complex than a bank account.

Workers and businesses would quickly adapt to this new configuration of green-bank accounts, as it allows them to earn income. The primary appeal is financial gain, not environmental activism. The green-market will succeed if people can manage their finances and bank accounts independently, without excessive government oversight or bureaucratic interference.

Tax-free: Minimal impact on the Treasury

The development of the green-market should not be hindered by concerns over potential tax revenue losses. First, any perceived shortfall could be offset by economic gains from job creation and higher wages within this new market, which would reduce reliance on welfare programs. Second, green products are currently relatively scarce, and a significant tax shortfall is unlikely given that the small number of corporations that have transitioned to green energy represents only a minor share of the IRS's tax base.

The green-market could also replace existing subsidy programs, which are being phased out as they lose political support due to their inefficiencies and limitations:

1: Cost to the government: Subsidies can strain the treasury if they exceed the difference between tax revenues included in the prices of green-products and those associated with goods powered by gasoline or natural gas. Caution: green subsidies are not generously offered by governments, as they rarely offset the numerous taxes included in the prices of green-products; and, when they do, governments are merely returning what they have collected elsewhere.

2: Bureaucratic complexity: The intricate subsidy application and approval process can be overwhelming, often discouraging small businesses and households from applying.

3: Favoring the wealthy: Amortizing the cost of solar panels requires a long-term commitment to recover the investment, even with subsidies. This can discourage struggling businesses and individuals, unlike wealthier households with a more secure financial future.

4: Arbitrary amounts loosely linked to carbon reductions: Subsidies do not always result in a lower carbon footprint.

5: Politicized or "picking market winners and losers": Governments may design subsidy programs that favor products manufactured in politically favorable precincts.

6: "Market distortion": Subsidies that guarantee a fixed purchasing price for green electricity over a 10-year period may unintentionally discourage energy producers from investing in cost-reduction improvements. This can create market price distortions, where subsidized prices remain higher than those in a competitive, unsubsidized market. However, this observation is less relevant for one-time subsidies for residential solar panel installations, where numerous service providers compete for swift project execution.

In response to these criticisms, subsidies are being reduced year after year, especially as renewable power plants and electric vehicles are becoming competitive without government support. Governments are even considering eliminating all subsidies and replacing them with a carbon tax to discourage the use of fossil fuels and continue to accelerate the green transition.

With subsidies likely to be phased out and no other clear method to untax clean energy, governments are left with energy-efficiency standards and carbon taxation schemes designed to reduce emissions in a market-friendly way. However, stringent regulations and carbon pricing mechanisms, such as the EU Emissions Trading System, have produced limited results in lowering emissions while also placing a disproportionate burden on low-income households. These policies have had minimal impact on job creation and carbon reduction and should be reconsidered.

A key issue with strict energy standards and carbon taxation is that low-income households allocate three times more of their budget to energy costs compared to higher-income households (source: US Department of Energy). Additionally, industries such as mining face the risk of job losses. While some subsidies attempt to offset these costs, they are often inaccessible to those who exceed income thresholds. As a result, low-income workers bear the greatest burden of carbon regulations, leading many to support politicians who oppose such measures. This resistance has made it difficult to sustain energy regulations, and any proposed carbon taxation bill is widely viewed as politically unviable in the US Congress.

A tax-free parallel system could offer a solution by shifting the focus from penalties to incentives. Instead of imposing energy regulations and carbon taxes, this approach would create jobs and encourage tax-free production.

2. A New Gray-Money to Supervise the Green-Market

A new gray-money within green-accounts

The price in green-money should not be viewed as a gauge of carbon consumption from fossil energy in the manufacturing of end products. Instead, the primary purpose of green-money is to provide a tax-exempt advantage, encouraging the consumption of environmentally friendly green-products. That said, the development of a carbon footprint indicator is still feasible and could be integrated within the green-accounts.

A gray-dollar could strengthen the system as a carbon gauge. This complementary unit would be symbolized by the color gray, evoking crude oil or anthracite coal. The color-coding feature would integrate with green-banking software. Bank engineers would create two separate transaction databases: one for green-currency and one for gray-currency. As with traditional currencies, these units would never mix and could only be exchanged for one another in currency markets. The green-money and gray-money systems would leave the regular dollar-based banking software untouched. They would largely mirror existing banking infrastructure, with one key modification: the introduction of new symbols to replace the familiar "$."

It would be strongly recommended that banks merge both accounts into a single, user-friendly interface. This integration would simplify the customers' management of the new dual-currency green-accounts. In this context, green-accounts would imply handling both green- and gray-currencies.

Introduction of gray-cents

Initially, gray-money, like green-money, would be exchanged for regular dollars at Federal Reserve counters. Subsequently, a symbolic tax of a few gray-cents could replace a portion of the existing federal excise taxes on each sale of a gallon of gas or a few pounds of coal. This distinctly visible carbon tax in gray-cents would equate one gallon of gas with 8.5 pounds of coal, as one gallon of gasoline emits approximately the same amount of CO_2 as 8.5 pounds of coal, according to the EPA. The same principle would apply to other greenhouse gas sources, such as gallons of butane, gallons of liquid hydrogen derived from natural gas, or megawatt-hours of electricity from coal power plants.

In response to this new symbolic carbon tax in gray-money, petroleum and coal producers would implement gray-money accounting alongside their standard financial reporting. This adaptation would enable them to start billing each unit of gas or coal in both currencies. Similar to operations in the regular and black markets, billing in two currencies should not disrupt corporations, as they are often capable of managing dual accounting systems.

Coal and oil industries would include the gray-cents collected within the federal excise tax payments to the IRS for each gallon of gas or pound of coal sold. The IRS would then be authorized to exchange its gray-money for regular dollars at the Federal Reserve, thereby restoring the income from the excise tax in regular dollars. This system would indirectly provide precise measurements of domestic CO_2 emissions from fossil fuels on a monthly basis.

Tracking fossil fuel consumption with gray-cents for voluntary corporations

Corporations committed to achieving carbon neutrality may choose to integrate gray-cents into their pricing. These corporations could market their carbon-neutral processes, potentially increasing their market share. This decision might be driven by growing consumer demand for transparency, with clear gray-cent pricing labels on store products.

These participating corporations would open a green-account to manage the gray-currency and ensure that gray-cents cannot be converted into regular dollars. Purchases made partially in gray-cents could only be offset by sales that also include gray-cents, with no way around this due to the nonexistence of physical gray-money banknotes. Alternatively, gray-cents could be managed through loans that must eventually be repaid via sales in gray-cents. Corporations would then adhere to the gray-cents system to account for, label, and sell their products at a hybrid price—combining both standard dollars and gray-cents—thereby enabling the tracking of the coal and gas consumption embedded in their products.

Reluctant downstream corporate consumers of petroleum and coal would have the right to ignore their carbon footprint. The accounting of gray-cents would be voluntary. These non-participating corporations would simply pay all excise taxes on fossil fuels, with their credit cards automatically handling any necessary currency exchange for gray-cents, as is currently done for international payments. Of course, these corporations could always change their minds if their consumers explicitly demanded the option to pay in gray-cents.

Easier control of green-corporations: Gray-cents fit perfectly with green-money

The use of gray-cents for regulatory control would be mandatory for green-corporations that have voluntarily entered the green-market. It is crucial to remember that the green-market is tax-free in exchange for strict auditing. Green-corporations are not authorized to resell non-compliant products tax-free.

Regulatory oversight is automated through the banking system, ensuring that the input of fossil fuels is accurately accounted for in the labeling of all output sales. Matching in-and-out flows between bank accounts would suffice, making this process less cumbersome than a bureaucratic eco-friendly regulatory code.

High prices in gray-cents or the accumulation of debts in gray-cents would expose unscrupulous green-corporations or their suppliers with high fossil fuel usage. The worst polluters among green-corporations could face gray-cent insolvency as authorities expel them from the green-market, or as consumers shift their preferences toward cleaner green-products.

Unlike untraceable black-market transactions, carbon cheating by green-corporations would be difficult to conceal. In this sense, gray-cents are a perfect complement to green-money, ensuring transparency and accountability.

Gray-cents for individuals: Eye-opening

At the end of the consumption chain, individuals and households would have the option to pay with gray-cents, following any necessary currency exchange. If they choose to disregard the green-market, any purchase in gray-cents would be automatically converted into dollar-cents by their credit card provider or by the cashier if paying with dollar bills.

Those opening a green account that handles both gray and green currencies could estimate the carbon footprint associated with their total gray-cent spending, which reflects their direct or indirect consumption of fossil fuels. These individuals could even obtain an accurate carbon footprint provided they purchase exclusively from corporations participating in the gray-cent system. Such gray-money amounts would serve as a highly precise tracker of fossil fuel emissions for each consumer.

To streamline transactions, participants could use a smartphone payment app or a dual-currency credit card. These payment tools would draw upon regular dollars from the conventional account and gray-cents from the green-account. The payment app or credit card software could even estimate CO_2 emissions linked to transactions from non-participating corporations, using a symbolic conversion to gray-cents—potentially overestimated to ensure climate safety—providing a view of the carbon footprint.

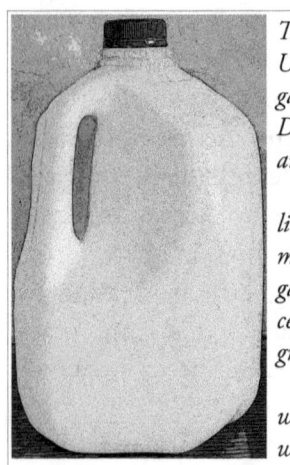

There is about half a pound of CO_2 emissions per dollar of US GDP according to the World Bank, while burning a gallon of gasoline releases about 20 pounds of CO_2 emissions. Derived from these figures, a rough estimate suggests that around 40 dollars of GDP is generated per gallon of gasoline.

Therefore, if 40 gray-cents are taxed on each gallon of gasoline, there would be about 1 gray-cent per dollar of output made from scratch in the US. According to this number, a gallon of milk (picture) could be priced at $4 and 5 gray-cents, but another brand could be priced at $5 and only 4 gray-cents.

This scenario poses an intriguing question: which bottle would the eco-friendly customer choose? Is it possible that they would opt for the product with the smallest carbon footprint? The answer can only be determined through a tax-free green-money system, where both green-dollars and gray-cents work together for accurate traceability. This represents another key idea underpinning the system. Testing the system in a limited area will reveal its effectiveness. If it fails, the gray-cent tax can simply be reverted to regular cents in the excise tax.

Ratcheting up the tax in gray-cents? Maybe never

If the consumption of petroleum and coal products does not decrease rapidly enough, despite the establishment of a competitive green-market, it may become necessary to impose additional carbon penalties in full gray-dollars on these items to mitigate the impacts of global warming.

Any form of carbon pricing must be considered a last resort, as it may face resistance from the middle class. Hopefully, such drastic measures will not be necessary. Moreover, an alternative strategy could guide the green economy toward net-zero emissions: the implementation of gray-cent quotas.

3. Make the Rich Pay More

Quotas of gray-cents

The gray-cent concept could pave the way for implementing carbon quotas for individuals. Under this paradigm, a reasonable quota of gray-cents could be granted at no charge to each individual or household, but not to corporations. This quota could be determined from the data collected during the prior phase of voluntary gray-cent usage.

A quota of gray-cents would offer a significant advantage over carbon pricing: individuals could avoid penalties as long as they remain within their allotted quota. This approach would be more manageable for low-income households than for the wealthy, whose lifestyles often involve larger properties, private jets, and luxury yachts.

Quotas on consumption items and long-term assets

The quantification of consumption items like staple foods, electricity, or gasoline purchases can be readily accounted for in the monthly quota according to their cost in gray-cents.

For durable goods such as cars, housing, or sailboats, which have long-term consumption patterns, an equitable framework could address both new and existing assets that were not subject to gray-cent charges at the time of their purchase. Several compensation options could be considered:

• New constructions: These might be required to secure a loan in gray-cents to account for their construction carbon footprint.

• Existing assets: A simplified mechanism could apply, such as a retrospective construction tax based on criteria like the square footage of a home or the asset's cost relative to the GDP dollar per carbon output for past purchases.

• Daily or monthly cost: Potential buyers or renters should consider

energy efficiency, such as insulation quality and expected utility costs, when evaluating a property.
• Exemptions: Exemptions could be granted for smaller assets, including compact houses (e.g., 1,000 square feet for two people), smaller vehicles, or electric vehicles, recognizing their lower impact.

This approach aims to balance carbon footprint accountability across different asset classes while considering the historical context of their construction and usage.

Monitoring cash withdrawals from regular accounts

All participants in the gray-cent quota system would be required to use the designated gray-cent payment application. This system would need to monitor cash withdrawals from standard bank accounts to ensure that anonymous banknotes are not used for unauthorized fossil fuel purchases, such as filling a gas tank.

To enforce this, mobile payment applications could incorporate features to record purchases made with cash and even track GPS data related to vehicle or private jet usage to detect discrepancies in gray-cent consumption. Alternatively, a fuel-tracking device could be required for gas-powered vehicles, while electric vehicles would be exempt. Other monitoring solutions could also be considered. Tracking should be relatively straightforward, as gasoline is the only fuel that can be purchased with cash.

Cash transactions in bars, restaurants, and other small-scale purchases would not impact the quota system significantly due to their low volume of gray-cents. Businesses might also choose to reject cash payments if they need to account for and pass on their own gray-cent costs to consumers.

One last possible measure could be to limit participants in the gray-cent system to savings accounts only, eliminating access to regular checking accounts. A linked green account could then be required to pull transaction data from existing checking accounts, enabling cross-checking and monitoring of any unaccounted fossil fuel consumption.

Corporations: Just passing it on to consumers

Corporations would be unaffected by individual gray-cent quotas, as these quotas would only apply to consumers. This approach contrasts with carbon credit quotas under schemes like the EU ETS or WCI, which are applied to the production side, and whose costs from exceeding quotas are often discreetly passed on to consumers through higher prices.

Implementing this system of gray-cent quotas for individuals would require every corporation to trace gray-cents through mandatory green-accounts and incorporate their gray-cent costs as a distinct supplement to the selling price in regular dollars of every output.

Individuals, regardless of their wealth, would be unable to evade their quota allowances for hidden purchases, as they would have no way to obtain gray-cents under the counter and deposit them into their closely supervised gray-cent accounts. Regular bank accounts could also be accessed for quota controls. Participation in the green-market system would remain voluntary for most individuals, but it might involve multiple layers of oversight.

A market for unused quotas: make the rich pay

Only the wealthiest segment of the population would initially be pressured to enter the green-market system with green-accounts and gray-cent quotas. Initially, this group could be limited to regular users of private jets or luxury yachts powered by fossil fuels. Over time, regulations could expand to encompass 10% or more of the population with stricter quotas.

Affluent individuals would face fines in full dollars for their excessive carbon emissions, as measured by gray-cents exceeding their individual quotas. These fines could increase exponentially as the wealthy monopolize large quantities of scarce commodities or clean energy, ensuring compensation for others facing higher costs of limited resources. Importantly, such penalties on the wealthiest would impact their spending rather than their investments.

The administration collecting these penalties would allocate the funds to green projects or subsidies. Alternatively, the administration could use the money from these penalties to purchase unused individual quotas, resulting in full dollars credited for each leftover gray-cent transferred to the administration.

Instead of paying fines to an administration, individuals could trade unused quota allowances in a novel market between frugal households and high-consumption consumers. Affluent consumers could purchase unused gray-cent quotas from more restrained households using standard currency, paying a few dollars for each gray-cent. They could then spend these additional gray-cents to consume resources—such as private jet fuel—that exceed their initial gray-cent allowances.

Recent economic studies show that the top 10% of Americans account for 50% of all consumer spending, contributing to roughly 40% of greenhouse gas emissions. This raises an important question: Should this group continue to have the unchecked right to emit such a large share of pollution?

There is a strong case for requiring them to offset their disproportionate environmental impact. One approach could involve reducing their household energy use through measures like installing solar panels and battery storage systems. However, these efforts have limited impact when it comes to more carbon-intensive activities, such as private air travel. In such instances, financial compensation or other forms of carbon offset may be necessary to more fully address their environmental footprint.

Incentivizing participation: A $1,000 monthly bonus

Quotas could provide households with several hundred dollars per week, depending on income levels. If higher-income participants actively engage in the system, the combination of tax-free green-money, green-jobs, and sales of unused gray-cent quotas could generate substantial financial benefits. For low-income households, this could translate into monthly bonuses reaching several hundred dollars—or even exceeding $1,000—enhancing economic participation and financial stability.

Low-income households could be incentivized to join the green-market, conserve more energy, and invest in energy-efficient products to maximize proceeds from their unused quota allowances in their green-accounts.

Corporations, influenced by customer demand, may also join the green market, adopting its specific accounting system and pricing their products in gray-cents. To reduce their gray-cent pricing, corporations could improve product design, cost structures, and pricing strategies for gray-cent components. Ultimately, sufficient pressure for cheaper green products could delay the need to mandate participation in the green market for both corporations and individuals.

The green transition cannot be solely the responsibility of top earners and corporations funding the shift for wasteful consumers. Nor can it rely exclusively on carbon pricing for large emitters while continuously excusing individual emissions or discouraging small businesses from growing to avoid being classified as large emitters, which negatively impacts employment. The green market must involve individual responsibility to conserve energy and create jobs for all, ensuring a balanced and sustainable transition.

Conclusion:
A Monetary Solution to Reduce Inequalities and Contain Global Warming?

If readers are open to the idea of a secondary currency, recognize the role of parallel markets like the black market, and believe that tackling inequality and climate change requires moving beyond ineffective government regulations, they may see value in the *Green-Market System*.

If the concept holds up to their scrutiny, they might consider sharing it with others—or exploring *The History of Money for Understanding Economics*, which offers a deeper look at how monetary systems have evolved and the many alternative models tested throughout history.

Bibliography

The complete bibliography can be found in:
Lannoye, Vincent. The History of Money for Understanding Economics. 2015

Origin of illustrations:

[7] Author's collection	[13] public domain

p9...[7]
p11...[7]
p13...[7]
p15...[13]
p19...[7]
p20...[7]
p21...[7]
p24...[7]
p28...[7]
p32...[7]

www.ingramcontent.com/pod-product-compliance
Lightning Source LLC
Chambersburg PA
CBHW050306220526
45465CB00002B/847